HIDDEN
UNKNOWN TRUTH

HIDDEN UNKNOWN TRUTH

A GUIDE TO CONSCIOUSNESS, SPIRITUAL AWAKENING, AND THE JOY OF LIVING

EDWARD SCOTT

Edward Scott

Hidden Unknown Truth: A Guide to Consciousness, Spiritual Awakening, and the Joy of Living

Cover creation courtesy of Arc Manor, LLC

Editing courtesy of Lorraine Reguly from WordingWell.com

To my son,

Anything is possible if we let go of our limited thoughts about it.

Thank you for helping me to find where the Hidden Unknown Truth exists.

CONTENTS

Introduction	9
1: Motivation to Try a New Way	11
2: Consciousness	19
3: Meditation	27
4: Thought Patterns That Keep Us Stuck	33
5: Overcome Resentful Thoughts	37
6: Forgiveness and Living Guilt-Free	47
7: Learning to Give Rather Than Take	53
8: Trading Fear for Courage	59
9: Humility	67
10: Gratitude and the Joy of Living	75
11: Prayer and Faith	81
12: Spiritually Awakened	89
13: Achieve True Freedom	95
14: Daily Practice	101
15: Continue Our Journey	107

Introduction

Do We Have a Problem Here?

This guide explains how to become aware of repetitive thoughts and actions that keep us stuck, how to let them go, and how to relax into our lives. We will learn a process that is effective in solving all of our mind's problems. If we can grasp the simple yet very true concept that we create our own problems in life, and that we only have a problem if we think we have a problem, then we will be able to change our entire existence. We can achieve this without trying to rearrange our lives outwardly, the way we have always tried to, only later realize we are still not fulfilled. Our reality changes when we change our thoughts about it. Our attitude and actions follow along, automatically.

Through mindfulness, meditation, and some straightforward actions, we will awaken our spirit. There is an inner power that we can draw upon to sustain us and bring forth the freedom we have sought. Peace of mind is not a myth. We can access a calm and serene place within us, any time that we choose to do so. Finding our purpose, knowing what direction to take next in our lives, and contentment can be found in this place. This place exists between our thoughts. An abundance of wisdom, love, and power to carry us through flows from this place.

Let's ask ourselves, *Why we would want to quiet our minds? How that will solve all of our problems?* Then let us explore why and how to do this with a very simple process that can be done at any time, in any place. We will discuss how to master some main drivers of a chaotic mind, such as resentment, fear, guilt, and selfishness. These cause us undesirable emotions and an unpleasant experience during our lives, on a daily basis. They also cause us to react to outer circumstances without intelligence. We will then discuss some of the benefits of practicing the simple process of quieting our minds, which leads to freedom and joyous daily living.

Through our pathway to consciousness, spiritual awakening, and the joy of living, we can gain access to limitless love, our own true purpose, freedom from emotional pain, real peace of mind, and a true joy of living our lives. This can all be done with a simple daily practice that will literally change everything!

1: Motivation to Try a New Way

Is This All There Is?

Why are you reading this book? You may be searching for answers to life's meaning. You may be searching for freedom from what seems like one struggle after another. Maybe you want the noise in your mind to stop. Maybe you aren't quite satisfied with yourself, your circumstances, or your entire existence. If you are anything like me, you seek to quench what seems like an unquenchable thirst to be content, by searching and grasping at anything you can get your hands on. You're unconsciously yet desperately hoping that this next thing will bring meaning and true happiness into your life, so you can stop the repetitive cycle of grasping for a solution and ultimately failing to get what you seek. You may have recognized this futile approach to life and have sworn you wouldn't repeat this approach but have found that you cannot stop doing it. Or maybe you are in complete and utter despair and a sense of hopelessness follows you everywhere you go. Life just doesn't seem quite right. Something is a little off, isn't it? We can't quite put our finger on what is off, though.

The reason why I sought to find a new way to live was because I repeated the same behaviors throughout my life in an insane attempt to feel whole. I wound up with my face flat on the ground. The result rarely changed, time after time. The only change was in the length of the temporary relief I found. Failure after failure became the normal pattern. I sought to get what I thought I wanted, only to find out I didn't want it. I could never fill the endless pit inside of me. I felt out of place and alone. I saw no reason for living. There seemed to be no point to life. I walked around with a sense that my life was meaningless. I experienced one painful experience after another with only brief moments of superficial happiness or fleeting contentment. I became sick and tired of being sick and tired. I found myself hopeless and in the utter depths of despair. A heavy, dark loneliness that I would not wish on my worst enemy seemed to follow me wherever I went. I desperately needed answers. More than that, I needed a miracle. I was lost. Living felt like I was being punished for a horrible crime I had committed.

If you want to learn how to find true, love, peace, purpose, and contentment, then this is the guide for you. I'll give you some insight to what I have found and learned. I can now see and touch what I can only describe as heaven, at any time that I choose to, and I didn't have to go anywhere or change anything on the outside of me to find this beautifully amazing reality. The truth I have found and experience daily is that I only have difficulties if I think I do.

Countless situations exist that look like a problem are not problematic to me. Some fears that roll around in my mind on repeat include the following questions: What if I don't have enough to pay my bills? What if I lose the person I love the most? What if I die? What if my friends stop liking me? What if I fail? What if I don't have fun? What if I'm late? Sometimes undesirable events and thoughts occur, such as: I don't have enough to pay my bills this month, my dog has just died, that person doesn't really like me, I am late for my appointment again, I was treated unfairly, I missed my opportunity for love and success, and I have been traumatized physically or mentally. Those are just a few experiences that have occurred at different times in my life. I'm sure you can easily formulate your own list. One thing for certain most of the time is that the fear we have had never materialized. If we could count the times we have been afraid of an undesirable event taking place and compared that number to the times the undesirable event actually took place, it would surprise us. We would see that only a tiny fraction of the time does our fear become reality. The problem is that fear dictates our lives and is almost a delusion as it rarely materializes. Fear takes away the joy of living our lives.

You may be asking yourself, *How can anything I do take away the thoughts that generate fear within me? How can I cope with the overwhelming pain I am feeling right now because my worst fear has happened? How can anything in this book solve anything for me? I don't know what to do.* The truth is, just reading this book can't solve anything for you but taking action will.

Whatever your troubles may be at any given moment of your life, if the methods outlined in this book are followed, your troubles will be taken care of. Remember this statement: *The reason why I am applying this process to my life is because I am seeking a real, lasting positive change, a sense of true purpose, and sustainable unlimited power—and I am open to trying something new.*

When we feel loneliness, is this because we have become dependent upon or too attached to something outside of ourselves?

I have observed that when I am living in the hustle of everyday life, the feeling of emptiness is covered up. I think I am distracted from feeling this emptiness. I have also observed that when I am alone and relaxed, I sometimes feel that something is missing. I have noticed that when I become attached to one person when they are not complying with my demands for attention, the emptiness is amplified. I have also noticed that when I become attached to a thing or behavior and I am not able to use it for comfort, the feeling is amplified. When the sense of emptiness arises within me, is something telling me that I am over-dependant on a person, place, or thing? If this is true, then what should I depend on? What is the solution to bring my body, mind, and spirit into a healthy equilibrium?

Rather than try to change my dependence on people or things outside of me and fail at that, maybe I should look at it from another angle. As soon as I let go of something in the material world, my mind will start searching for another solution to satisfy it. This pattern has been in place for many years of my life. I've watched countless people exhibit similar behavior.

We try to solve our internal problems by seeking solutions in the material world. The general pattern goes something like this: we are not content, so we attempt to solve this by making an external change, we are temporarily satisfied, but our internal problems resurface. We continue this same behavior over and over and always end up back at our original problem. We're no further ahead.

What dependence should we really let go of? We

have tried everything we can think of to solve this gnawing sense that something isn't quite right within us. Our ideas tend to inevitably lead us right back to where we began. Could it be that our methods to gain a sense of security, purpose, and connection have been missing the mark? How much effort should we put into solving our inner struggle for contentment by focusing on how we should act in front of other people to gain approval, how we are living up to our values, the measurement of how others are living up to our values, and the measurement of how we are living up to others' values?

I know I have exerted an exhausting amount of effort seeking security, purpose, and connection in this way. I have spent the majority of my life trying to fit in. My inner problems arise when I don't seem to fit in—whether this is true or something I have imagined. Most of the time, it's imagined, and I act the way I think I should act, hoping for approval. When the approval comes, temporarily, I feel relief on the inside. My dependence on that euphoric feeling perpetuates my dependence on people, places, and things to bring me a sense of security and worthiness. My thought reals repeat the same list of things to worry about fixing while reassuring me that once they are fixed, I'll be content. Some of the standard thoughts I have including wondering if my house is nice enough, my lawn green enough, my child polite enough, my work admirable enough, or if I am funny enough. The list goes on forever! My ego tries to convince me that I am missing something and it focuses on finding the solution in the material world.

I don't think my ego is good or bad. It just *is*. My ego only knows what it knows from past experience. It searches for a solution by using any means necessary. It defaults to focusing on anything that ever brought any sort of relief to my inner being. The thoughts produced by my ego are not inherently bad, although sometimes they elicit bad advice. Whether I like it or not, I'm stuck with my ego, so I might as well make friends with it. Rather than ignore my ego or become angry with it, I have learned to acknowledge my ego's wants. When I acknowledge my thoughts, I can then move toward letting them go, if I choose to. I don't need to fit in to gain a sense of worth anymore.

I don't think there is anything wrong with fitting in with people. Relating with people is good and can provide a comforting sense of belonging and intimate connection, which we need. We all relate with people or groups of people on different levels. Some people we develop deep and meaningful connections with and others we do not. That is perfectly normal. The problem arises when we expect to fit in or expect to be accepted and that does not happen the way we would like it to happen. The problem is making "fitting in" the goal to strive for. There is everything right with creating our lives and living in the material world. Our problem is that we try too hard to gain inner contentment by attempting to fill the void with worldly things. The result is always the same—we're never further ahead than before we started. We end up feeling the empty void within us once again.

Let's explore a different set of daily practices that will show us how to gain a sense of security, purpose, and connection our inner being has been missing.

2: Consciousness

I Think, Therefore I Think

My biggest problem is the constant chatter in my mind telling me I have a problem. The simple truth is that *I only have a problem if I think I have a problem*. Our mind narrating possible future situations or reminding us that we have experienced an undesirable situation will not solve anything. Logically, we can see that we only have a problem if we view it as a problem. *I am only afraid if I think I am afraid!* That is easy for us to see. Our reality is filtered through our minds. If our minds could be hardwired to automatically look at a situation and then relay it to us as, *This is an amazing situation and I am very excited about it*, we would never have a problem. Obviously, that is not realistic to expect, is it? Yet, this concept is a truth. We only have a problem if we think we have a problem. That is a fact.

The real problem that we have is a lack of awareness of our thoughts and emotions. Most of the time, we are unaware that we are thinking or feeling. I have spent the majority of my life completely identified with my thoughts and emotions. I used to *be* thoughts and emotions. They were me and they were real. My thoughts were the main driver of my emotions. When I felt an emotion, it reinforced my thoughts, which solidified my emotional response. When my emotion becomes strong enough, it takes over and my actions follow whatever it dictates. I spent years living completely unaware of this cycle. I was my thoughts and emotions. There was nothing else. The result of living with this ignorance was that I desperately grasped at anything outside of myself that I could get my hands on to help comfort me. I had no other truth to rely on except for my thoughts and emotions. The hidden unknown truth eluded me, day after day. Life was meaningless once all the distractions of the material world quieted down.

There is a fundamental concept that we are not our thoughts or emotions. We are the ones who can watch the thoughts and feel the emotions. Consciousness begins once we are aware that we are thinking or feeling. One day, I realized that I was thinking. It occurred to me that if I can see my thoughts, then what is watching them? I spent months going in and out of consciousness. I tried to watch my thoughts. Sometimes I was aware that I was thinking and sometimes I wasn't. It took practicing day after day before I realized that I am not identified with my thoughts if I am watching them. This meant that a thought was just a thought and I could choose whether I acted upon that thought or not. When I am not aware of my thinking, I have little power over my thoughts. The same is true about my emotions. I found that I could feel my emotions and see them for what they were—responses to the thoughts that occurred in my body. This was a revolutionary epiphany moment. It meant that there was something else inside of me that was able to watch my thinking. It also meant that when I was watching my thinking, I had a choice in which thought to let go of and which thought to process further.

We have no power over which thoughts enter our mind. However, we have power over what we decide to do with a thought, if we are aware of it. This is where change happens for us. When we are watching our thoughts and emotions, it means that we are in contact with something else inside of us. It means we have access to the power over our minds. This is the foundation required for enlightenment. Practicing watching our thoughts, emotions, and nothing else will change your life.

Here are some exercises to practice to help you become more aware of your thoughts and emotions as well as how to let them go as they arise.

Awareness of Our Thoughts

Look at any object that you can see right now. For example, I see a lamp. You can use any object. Once you have the object picked out, ask yourself how large the object is? Your mind may now try to calculate maybe the height, width, or weight of the object. Try to observe your mind thinking about the object. Ask yourself the question again and take a minute to think about the answer while watching your thoughts as they are happening. *How large is the object?*

Could you observe your mind thinking? I could. I can observe my mind thinking as I write this sentence. My mind is thinking! The first time I truly realized that I could watch my thoughts I wondered what, then, is watching them? The truth is that my true self is watching them. My higher mind —if we want to call it something—is watching my thoughts. The hidden unknown truth is watching my thoughts!

This concept is the foundation of this process. We want to practice becoming aware of our thoughts. We must do this, or change cannot happen. If we are not aware that we can watch our thoughts, we are not conscious and are, therefore, living in quite an unconscious state. We're ruled by our minds.

Practice watching your thoughts throughout the day. The more we do it, the more we awaken. As we practice, it becomes easier to watch our thoughts. Eventually, it becomes second nature. We're now on the path to consciousness, which simply means awareness!

Once we are aware of our thoughts, we have the choice of whether to let them go or not.

Let Go of a Thought

Letting go of a thought is a powerful skill to learn because a thought can affect how we perceive a situation, ourselves, others, and the world around us. It also can cause a feeling that will generate emotion in the body. Being able to let go of a negative thought has a great advantage for us. It can help us to enjoy life rather than struggle through it. The biggest benefit of having the skill to let thoughts go is that we can use this skill to be at peace. We can have access to an unlimited supply of power that flows from within us, which will enable us to truly live a fulfilling day, and ultimately, a fulfilling life! Using simple phrases, we can change how we interact with the world and ourselves, which will change everything about our lives.

When a thought occurs in your mind, acknowledge that the thought is present by saying in your mind *I see the thought*. Then accept the thought as just a thought by saying *I accept this thought as only a thought*. Finally, let it go by saying *I am letting the thought go*. When the next thought happens in your mind, repeat this process. Try this for 1 minute. Then try it for 5 minutes, a little later on. Set a timer on a clock to let you know when the time is up, then see how your mood is. Also take note of how your energy level is. I bet you'll notice a slight shift in your mood, a new perspective on the moment, and a slight rise in your energy.

23

Awareness of Our Emotions

This exercise takes practice and begins with becoming aware of how your body feels. Maybe we feel our heart beating faster if we are anxious or angry. Maybe our temperature is slightly higher, our ears are warm, or our face is flush if we are embarrassed. We may feel tightness in our shoulders or lower back if we are carrying stress. Maybe we feel lighter and euphoric when we feel infatuation or the signs of love. The key is to watch for emotions in our body by focusing on how our body feels. As soon as we become aware of an emotion and see it for what it is, just a sensation in our body, it loses all power over us.

Let Go of an Emotion

Once we get used to being aware of our emotions, we can then acknowledge the emotion and let it just be.

Sometimes it takes some time for the emotion to run its course. Some emotions are wonderful to experience and we enjoy them. Some emotions seem terrible to experience. Emotions (whether what we perceive as good or bad), when acted upon, often cause us trouble. I have learned to practice accepting the emotion as a sensation in my body. I do this by taking the risk of just feeling the emotion without acting on it. The key here is to feel the emotion fully, while watching how your body feels.

Focus on how your body feels rather than the thoughts that are driving the emotion. To let these emotions go, we acknowledge how our body feels and let it subside while also acknowledging, accepting, and letting any emotion-driven thoughts go. Do not act upon anything until the emotional response in your body has subsided. When we practice this, we prevent taking actions that could cause us to be sorry later on and we make much more intelligent decisions.

We have just discussed the foundation method to gain access to our hidden unknown truth, which is the awareness of our thoughts and emotions. When practicing these techniques, we automatically move much closer to accessing where limitless love, our true purpose, freedom from emotional pain, peace in our mind, and the joy of living our lives comes from. We are in contact.

Now, let us realize that connection on a deeper level by implementing mediation in our daily practice.

3: Meditation

Just Shut Up and Listen!

We know that something is watching our thoughts and emotions. This is the quiet voice that dwells within us. This watcher is us, as an expression of a higher power source. Some people call it their spirit. Others call it their intuition. Whatever name we assign to it, this "watcher" is actually our higher intelligence and it is void of ego. Pride doesn't live here; only the highest form of pure love lives here. It doesn't need thoughts to live as our ego does. This quiet voice doesn't repeat the same futile attempts to become contented as our ego does; it is contentment itself.

We want to bring the hidden unknown truth about us to the surface and follow its direction from now on. It is everything we need and has everything we need. How do we make the quiet watcher louder than our ego's thoughts? The first step is awareness of our thoughts and emotions. The second step is letting them go. The third step is listening to the quiet voice regularly.

To do this, we apply a simple process of quieting our thoughts down. We can affect a change in our perception about the problems that our thoughts remind us about every single day of our lives. We can apply this process of quieting our thoughts to large or small problems. The result of quieting our thoughts allows for a different voice to begin dominating our minds. When our quiet voice is no longer hidden behind our loud rambling thoughts, our entire existence will change and we won't have any more problems—only a hundred situations that look like problems.

My first attempt at meditation came after I began watching my thoughts. I realized that my thoughts never stopped. The loud voice in my mind couldn't seem to shut up, so I started searching for a solution to my chattering mind. It did not take much research to realize that meditation could help me with my thinking problem. I looked for meditation methods and read that it only takes a couple of minutes per day of meditation to find peace of mind. I then decided to meditate for two minutes each day, although I initially had no idea how to meditate. At that time, I had an electric fireplace in my living room. The fake flames that it produced were hypnotic. I began by setting a two-minute timer and I stared at those flames, trying my best not to think. It didn't take long to learn that trying not to think is like trying not a put your hands out to break your fall if you slip. I also realized that two minutes felt like an eternity. It was agonizing to just sit there with my thoughts, yet I was determined to continue. I did this day after day, for months. After a little while, it became easy to sit for two minutes. Quieting my thoughts seemed impossible until I picked a point to focus on. Each time I trailed off into my thoughts, I returned to the focal point, which was my breath. Quieting my thoughts through meditation eventually became a simple process.

I begin meditation by sitting comfortably and breathing in and out. I focus on the feeling of my breath going in and out from my body. That is my initial focus. Thoughts come into my mind and I practice letting them go and returning my focus onto the breath. Eventually, the thoughts subside and I reach a place where there is nothingness, which becomes my next focal point. The only way I can describe the experience of being focused on the nothingness is that I feel as though my mind is being released from all tension, followed by a sense of freedom. It feels like a breath of fresh air on a crisp autumn morning that is surrounding me. There is no fear, anger, guilt, happiness, or excitement. It just is. It is peaceful and invigorating. The best thing about this is that this state of being is accessible at any time, in any place.

The longer we can be at peace, the better it gets. From there, true creativity is born. Answers to problems will come... not always during the meditation, but afterward. As we continue throughout our day, the solution to any obstacles in our path will be revealed. Our thinking slows down and we become much more intuitive. Once we have established contact with this place, as the day goes on, we can easily go back to this place of comfort that brings such peace and freedom. We can begin to consciously think, rather than just think unconsciously while reacting to situations, thoughts, or emotions. We can use our minds rather than have our minds control us. We can choose what to think about. We can choose to let go of the stories that we make up in our minds that cause fear, worry, anger, unreasonable expectations, or anything troublesome. A higher intelligence takes over that allows us to function more efficiently, without having to think incessantly. We think and act more with inspiration and love, rather than fear. It's a revolutionary change!

This simple process can be summarized into five easy meditation steps:

1. Get Comfortable—Close your eyes and sit comfortably anywhere. Sit as relaxed as you can.

2. Set the Stage—Keep this simple, by telling yourself *I have absolutely nothing to do other than be here right now*. If desired, set a timer for a few minutes or longer to help with getting used to setting aside time for meditation.

3. Breathe—Inhale while focusing on the feeling of your breath entering your body. Feel the cool air passing by your lips or nostrils and entering your lungs. Exhale while focusing on the feeling of warmth flowing out through your lips or nostrils.

4. Let Go—When you notice yourself thinking instead of focusing on your breathing, say in your mind *I see the thought, I accept the thought, and I'm letting the thought go*. As you say this to yourself, focus on your breath each time. When the thoughts slow down, keep breathing. Soon, all thoughts are gone, except for a distant sense that maybe you are thinking. Continue this until you feel the tension in your mind being released.

5. Relax—Relax into the quietness and continue to experience nothing but what is between your thoughts. Continue to experience the release from tension in the mind, which almost feels like taking a breath of fresh air. When the urge to get up and go arises, acknowledge, accept, and let it go and stay in this place for a few moments or minutes longer. Relax; you have nowhere to go. Enjoy this peaceful and comfortable place.

They say that "practice makes perfect," but "practice makes better"! Meditation is a skill that is both challenging and very rewarding. You will find that you do not create trouble when you return to a calm state before acting on any emotion, whether good or not so good. You will also see that when you fail to let your thoughts and emotions pass, you create your troubles. When that happens, it is a good reminder of why you began this daily practice in the first place. That failure will help you to try once again to practice calming your mind, so you can experience peace of mind and the release from tension once again.

Next, let's explore how to make further room for our hidden unknown truth to shine through us by examining the major thought processes that stand in our way of conscious contact with our inner truth.

4: Thought Patterns That Keep Us Stuck

Iceberg Straight Ahead!

We tend to hold onto thoughts about experiences we have had and use those thoughts to predict experiences we may have in the future. This brings us into a fantasy land in our minds. Our imagination can be fired up and we can take steps to pursue a small goal or a lifelong dream because of this ability. Unfortunately, we also tend to relive past troubles we have experienced and imagine how we'll meet new troubles as we move forward in our lives. Whatever the case is (either good or bad), this keeps the noise in our minds constantly humming. We need to deal with the cause of our recurring thoughts or they will keep coming back to haunt us.

There are four major categories to look at: resentment, guilt, selfishness, and fear. Resentment is re-thinking about a past hurt which causes us to re-feel it. Guilty thoughts are caused by thinking about what we perceive as past mistakes. Selfishness is focusing on ourselves without consideration for anybody or anything else. Fear is the anxiety we feel about how we will be affected in the future because of these other three thought patterns. Fear is the result of resentment, guilt, and selfishness. As it turns out, fear is also the cause of resentful, guilty, and selfish thought patterns. We cannot have one without the other.

This is a case of the chicken, the egg, and which came first. For example, if I expected nothing, wanted nothing, and needed nothing, would I feel fear? Logically speaking, I would have no fear. When we look at it from another angle, would I be resentful of somebody if I had no fear that they seem to be getting away with hurting me? Would I be afraid to meet the person that I harmed in the past if I didn't feel guilty about my actions? Whether or not fear is the cause or the effect of selfish, resentful, and guilty thoughts or not is irrelevant. Fear is involved in all of them. Fear appears to be the cause and effect of the other three thought patterns. Actually, all four of these categories overlap each other. Fear dictates our negative recurring thoughts and actions—and ultimately, the course of our lives, if we allow it to continue.

For a moment, imagine what your life would be

like without these perpetual thought patterns constantly rolling around in your mind. A quick experiment to try is to apply the process of quieting your mind for a few minutes. Follow the five steps outlined in **Chapter 3: Meditation**. When we quiet down, there is less identification with our thoughts. We're no longer on autopilot, following the dictations of our thoughts. We are free, so inspiration and love can flow through us. We want for nothing in those moments. We are completely satisfied with everything at that exact moment. It's a beautiful gift. Ask yourself, *Do I want or need anything that I don't already have right in this very moment?*

Now, imagine walking around, daily, aware of those thoughts, knowing the thoughts themselves cannot harm you in any way, and that you don't have to take any action from them. Imagine knowing that you can do what you've always secretly wished you could do, despite believing that you were **not good enough** to do because of the guilt of falling short in life and relationships, that you are **a coward** (because of fear), that you're not a **kind enough** person (because of selfish inconsideration), or that you've **been dealt a bad hand in life** (because of resentment). The list of reasons can go on forever. Imagine what life would be like without these lies dominating your thinking (which, inevitably, dictates your actions)!

Take a moment to ponder whether your life problems are caused by these thinking patterns or not. Remember, *we only have a problem if we think we have a problem*.

When you are ready, dig deeper into these four main destructive, emotion driving, and blocking thought patterns by reading the chapters that follow.

5: Overcome Resentful Thoughts

Resentment Is Futile

What is resentment and why do we care about it? Resentment simply means to re-feel. Resentful thoughts come in the form of anger, remorse, or just plain fear.

For example, I've told somebody something in confidence and then the person turned around and told other people our conversation. Initially, I felt extremely angry. Underneath that, I felt betrayed and just plain hurt. I trusted that person. A day later, I thought about that event and I became angry toward that person again and re-felt the feelings I felt initially. This is the beginning of resentment.

Each time I re-feel an event, typically one that I perceive as negative and toward a person or group of people, that's resentment. If we look carefully and maybe think for a couple of minutes, we may find the resentments we have. If we cannot see any, let's take the next day to watch our thinking. We're sure to see that there is somebody who crops up in our thinking from the past day or week, or from years ago, and we think, *How dare that person! Why would they do that to me*? That is resentment.

What is at the root of the resentment? First of all, we're blaming somebody else or a group of people (such as a past employer, the government, or our significant other) for harming us. That is clear. But what drives this resentment? Why does it keep coming back and why do we re-feel the emotions from an event that happened in the past?

I feel fear when I make mistakes that somebody may be hurt or upset with me, so when it happens to me, I blame people for their flaws to cover up my fear. Then I replay this over and over, depending on how my behavior has been and how much fear I'm feeling about my behavior.

The reason I access this instant replay is to help me feel better about me and how I am acting is because I'm afraid. I have a fear that maybe I'm not perfect. When harm (small or large) happens, and I am in the path of it, I grab a hold of that and use it to comfort me because I make mistakes sometimes. I'm missing the mark just like every other person on the planet. Yet, when I make a mistake and harm somebody unintentionally, I feel guilty, remorseful, sad, compassionate, and so on. To counteract these feelings, I look for the way that I was harmed and blame others so I don't have to look at or feel my own mistakes. I do it unconsciously; I'm not aware that I do this. Yet it is counterproductive and spiritually draining for all involved. Resentment is simply a tool to help me feel better about me.

Resentment is a problem for us, for many reasons. Firstly, it generates negative thoughts and emotions that are not healthy for our bodies or our state of mind. Secondly, it keeps our minds living in fear and denying our mistakes, which prevent us from learning from them and growing in regards to living in harmony with other people. Thirdly, we get stuck in the past and in our minds, which wastes our days. How can we walk forward in life if we are constantly looking backward? Another major reason and the most important is it keeps our minds constantly distracted and cuts us off from the inner inspiration and intelligence that flows out through us. We are cut off from that energy source. We are cut off from true peace of mind. Resentment is truly useless; it's futile!

What can we do about our resentments?

They are not healthy for us, in the slightest. They

don't provide any benefit other than keeping us living in denial and trapped in our minds. They perpetuate us to live in a never-ending circle of repeating those same behaviors that cause our troubles. They prevent intellectual, emotional, and spiritual growth. They are a major blockage that we need to get rid of. Do we really want to be angry this much about the past? I know that I don't!

One thing we need to realize about others is that they are probably doing the absolute best that they can, at any given time, just like we are. If we can look at people as doing the absolute best they can, it helps us to acknowledge the hurt, accept it, and let it go. We could have possibly made a mistake sometime in our lives, too, and I'm sure we would want the person we unintentionally wronged to not resent us!

Some people or groups may be extremely harmful or sick or even appear evil. How can we accept behaviors we see in others that we would never dare do? This one takes a little more effort, especially if we have been harmed greatly or if somebody close to us has been hurt badly in a way we couldn't comprehend. We might ask ourselves, *Why would somebody hurt someone else like that?*

I've been hurt quite badly by somebody. For years I held onto some heavy pain. I was resentful and blamed others for my pain and I stayed stuck in it. I became spiritually sick because of this resentment.

It was affecting my daily life. Life appeared to be a struggle and bleak. Then I realized was that maybe the person who caused the harm was hopelessly sick while the events took place, or perhaps they were harmed greatly in a similar manner. Maybe the person became so sick that they couldn't help the action. When I began to view the person as possibly being physically, mentally, or spiritually very sick, I began to have compassion. I felt bad for the person and felt pity. I started to see that I was living in constant fear because of my resentment, and that my fear of being hurt was preventing me from connecting with people on a deeper level. Once I realized that because of my fear, I was creating my own problems by pushing people away, the resentment began to dissolve from that place of understanding.

Sometimes, we can or need to write about the resentment, if it is deep-seated, using a simple exercise where we state what the resentment is and where we could have possibly been to blame. For example, maybe I directly harmed the very same person who harmed me and they lashed out at me out of sheer frustration. Maybe, indirectly, my fear of intimacy was causing people to keep their distance from me. This brings some truth back into the resentment, because typically each time I re-feel an event, it becomes more and more the other person's fault (or the group's fault) and less my fault. We can list a few short points about what the resentment is and then try to find where we played a part in it.

In another example, a person made fun of me in front of others for making a mistake at work. It embarrassed me. I quietly took offense and immediately began picking that person apart in my mind. I left the group discussion and kept my distance from that person for days, which turned into weeks.

Where is my part in this? It's simple: I disengaged from the group out of embarrassment and then became more upset because I wasn't included in the group conversations as much when the offending person was around. My standoffish attitude toward the person could have given the impression that I was sour, which may have triggered fear or resentment in them as well.

I have also made fun of somebody in front of other people before. Just like the person I resent, I'm capable of the same action. Perhaps our part may be that we are re-feeling something to the point where it's making us sick. Maybe we have never done anything close to how we were treated, so looking at how we talk about the event and how it's hurting us is our part to play.

We should also realize that we create our own misery because we are reliving something that the other person (or people) may not even know about. They may not know they harmed us. So, we are hurting ourselves over and over, inadvertently, and we are also hurting others because of the fear we have of being hurt again.

Should we let the past event dictate our present lives? Of course, we shouldn't! Instead, we should let go of our resentments. The method to get rid of resentment is as follows:

1. Awareness—Remind yourself that everybody is doing the absolute best they can. Also, realize that we also make mistakes because we are flawed.

2. Alternate Perspective—Remind yourself that maybe the person is or was very physically, mentally, or spiritually sick during the time they harmed you. This will help you to develop compassion. Consider what they could have had on their plate that day. Maybe they were going through a tough time and took their frustrations out on you. Take some time and contemplate this the next time somebody crosses you. Maybe the person who cut you off in traffic just lost a loved one so dear to them that their will to live is hanging by a thread. Maybe they are on auto-pilot, trying to take care of funeral arrangements while consoling their other loved ones and keeping the daily needs of their family flowing.

3. Acknowledgment—Write about it and realize that you will be okay. This is the key to being free from the spiritual, life-sucking disease of resentment. Answer these four questions specifically: What am I upset about? How do I feel? Have I ever done the same to anybody else or similar? Did I ever cause any harm (minor or major) to this person or anybody else because of my actions?

Regardless of your answers and the reason why somebody hurt you, you will be okay. During the times that resentment arises within me, I say to myself, *I am okay and will be okay*.

4. Let Go—After you acknowledge the resentment, you can accept it and let it go—just as you would with a thought. Repeat this over and over, each time it arises in your thinking. This may take as little as a few moments or days and possibly up to a couple of weeks. As you continue this step, you will notice that the blockage of the resentment will be eventually cleared and you'll be free of it.

5. Give—A quick and highly effective tactic to clear resentment without much effort is to do something kind for the person who has crossed you. This is good for those petty, daily resentments we pick up with friends, family, and coworkers. As soon as I do something small for the offending person, my resentment evaporates. I offer to buy the offender a coffee or to help them with something small they may need a hand with.

When we can admit our part or our wrongdoing in the event that causes the resentment, we have grown. When we can let go of our thoughts about the resentment and think honestly about the event or situation, we have grown. As we grow, our be-haviors will change for the better. We will feel more peace in our minds and our energy level will rise. The solution to any resentment is really sim-ple: overcome your resentful thoughts by using the process outlined in this chapter. Remember, resent-ment is futile, and this process works!

6: Forgiveness and Living Guilt-Free

Guilty Until Proven Guilty

My mind will often distract me with guilt from actions wherein I might have caused a disturbance in somebody else. For example, at times, I like to prove I'm right and may force my opinion onto somebody else in a conversation just to satisfy my ego's thinking. I may completely disregard the other person's view on the matter and not have an open heart to truly hear the message that they are trying to transmit about the subject. Besides the fact that I am being inconsiderate, arrogant, and controlling (by forcing my belief onto the person), I am also missing out on valuable information and possibly a much greater truth than I have.

Depending on the impact of the harm I may have

caused, the thoughts about the interaction some-times resurface in my thinking, causing me to feel guilty. This guilt may come back indefinitely if I do not deal with it. Recurring guilt can be a continuous distraction in my mind and it affects how I interact with people and myself. Guilt holds me back from true connection with other people. Guilt is also a good indicator that I have missed the mark with living my values.

How can we deal with this guilt? Becoming aware of the guilt we carry will help us to act according to our values. Awareness is also the key to let it go and be free of it for good. Recurring guilt can be a major distraction in our lives and another major blockage for us. We must find a way to clear away any guilt that we carry with us.

I have found that I am guilty until proven guilty. Once I honestly acknowledge that I was wrong, the guilt begins dissipating immediately. Once I investigate and notice that this sort of situation keeps arising, I'll listen to the other person's viewpoint and engage in a constructive (rather than destruct-ive) conversation, the guilt dissipates. Sometimes, it disappears completely! There have been cases where I had to go much further and approach the individual and admit my wrongdoing honestly, then ask for forgiveness. This usually takes any lin-gering guilt away. It also allows the other person the option of opening and releasing any of their re-sentment, which unblocks them from accessing the

beautiful peace of mind where inspiration and intuition meet to form a romance made in heaven!

The answer to guilt is restitution. Restitution
means to restore something to its original state
or to right the wrong, by admitting our mistakes
to both ourselves and another trustworthy person.
Then, depending on the cause of the guilt, we can
make restitution to the person we harmed (if it's
possible) and not repeat the harm, moving forward.
The solution to any guilt is simple: think of restitution and apply the following three steps:

1. Awareness—Practice watching for guilt. When
you see something you feel guilty about, you can
write it down in point form. This helps take it out of
your mind and it also removes any denial you have
about it. This is a powerful and easy tool you can
use to counteract the sometimes bombardment of
guilty thoughts.

2. Restitution—Think of how to fix your wrongdoing and move toward correcting it by either admitting your fault to the person you have wronged
or correcting the mistake you have caused by not
repeating it as you move forward.

3. Let Go—When guilt crops up, say to yourself, *I
acknowledge that I am guilty. I accept it. I am letting
it go*. You can also ask your inner self for forgiveness
for originally missing the mark.

We're all human and sometimes we make mis-

takes. As soon as we start to move toward the solution of restitution, the guilt subsides and we become free.

I have found that once somebody acknowledges
how they have wronged me, any resentment I have
toward them often vanishes and I become unblocked. I have asked people that I have amended
my wrongs with if they, too, felt differently afterward, and have been told that their ill feelings toward me subsided or vanished as well. This is great
news and is proof that these three steps work effectively.

When we own our mistakes and honestly and
openly try to correct them, we unblock not only
ourselves but other people as well. We begin to
balance the spiritual scales and contribute to this
world more.

The key to how to forgive ourselves and other
people is by amending our own mistakes as we go.
If we follow the process in this chapter honestly
and thoroughly, we will forgive all those who ever
wronged us and we'll also forgive ourselves for our
own mistakes.

We're performing selfless acts when we are honest
about our mistakes and when we accept respon-
sibility for them. We become free from guilt and
remorse as we open up the channel to something
much better. We help the other person (or people)

involved by helping to clear their mind(s) from re-sentment, which helps to open their heart(s) as well.

Each time we let go of past guilt, it's one less dis-traction in our minds and one less recurring emo-tional response to the guilty thoughts. The clearer our minds are, the healthier we are.

Accessing the hidden unknown truth becomes easier and easier, allowing us to be in the present moment and all of its beauty more frequently, and for longer periods. We can then function on a much higher level of existence where true intelligence, inspiration, creativeness, joy, and love exist.

7: Learning to Give Rather Than Take

Selfish Is As Selfless Does

I believe we are all capable of selflessness despite the general selfishness of our thoughts. In this chapter, we will examine how our thinking can be switched by putting the focus on thinking about—and acting on—how we can give.

When I monitor my thoughts, I see a pattern. They are typically, in some form or another, about me. They may be dressed up to look like they point outward, away from me, to other people or causes, but if I trace them back to the fear, excitement, or even comforting feelings, they always point back to me. Many of my thoughts are ultimately selfish, to some degree. ***How will this next adventure or task or event affect me?***

I also have some automatic, selfless thoughts based on my love for somebody (such as my child or best friend, for example). Those thoughts come from my instincts; from an inner place where true love lives. When an emergency happens, I instinctively go into a mode of trying to preserve another's life or well-being. This is a natural type of reaction for all of us, which reinforces my belief that we are all capable of selflessness.

However, I have noticed that most of my thoughts are about me. Those thoughts dictate my emotions and actions. *Will I be late for work? Where are my keys? What will my boss say about my performance? I'll be embarrassed if I am late for that meeting. What will they say about me?* And so on. My emotions will drive my thoughts more and I'll begin to feel anxious or angry, impatient, frustrated, or overwhelmed. This is a major distraction! It is a perfect setup to keep me thinking selfishly—and away from the hidden unknown truth.

What I have learned through years of thinking selfishly is that I am constantly distracted. I also have discovered that thinking mainly about myself consistently makes my life a lot less enjoyable. It's like I am constantly walking around with proverbial binoculars on limiting my point of view or attitude that "I know what is best for me and everybody else," and it's very lonely at the top when I'm trying to play God from my mind. My sense of purpose was subpar, at best, even though I used to think I was, for the most part, selfless. When I began watching my thoughts regularly and reviewing my actions, I was able to see my thoughts and actions and the negative emotion that hummed constantly in the background. I then realized that I was quite self-focused and I needed a way to quiet my mind down. The solution was to, again, acknowledge the selfish thought, accept it, and let go. That process allowed me to begin consciously thinking about other people and finding ways to serve them to improve their lives as my main motive. When I think about how I can help others (including you), I have a purpose!

Selfishness blocks us from attaining a true peace of mind and ultimately from that almost imaginary thing we call happiness. Selflessness does for others and removes the distracting thoughts and emotions that block us from being truly free. When I think outside of me and do for others, I am free from worry and my problems. It provides genuine usefulness and purpose to my life when I give to others through thought and action. This may already be a regular activity for some of us, a new adventure for others, and some people might even be somewhere in between. The truth I know right now is that the more I think about others and how I can meet their needs and act upon that, the more I receive internally. It clears my mind, almost like a magic trick. This action removes the gut-wrenching sense that I have no real purpose or point to being here. It fills the endless pit of nothingness. So, I remind myself that I am here to serve rather than to be served. I have realized that the more I do this, the more I gain mentally, physically, and spiritually. Don't worry about becoming completely selfless and not having your needs met. Instinctively, we will maintain our own needs. In fact, my own experience is that the more I think and act selflessly, the more my needs are met. I have also noticed that I gained the invaluable human need for companionship in the process.

The answer to selfishness is striving for selflessness while accepting we may never achieve this perfect ideal. How can we accept that we will never achieve the perfect ideal? The way to accept anything is through honesty. If I look at anything I struggle with as honestly as I can, acceptance will come. In this case, all of the evidence of my entire life, what other people have shared, and what I have witnessed shows me that I will never achieve perfect selflessness. I accept this fact but I still try my best to walk toward this ideal.

The solution to any selfishness is simple, although it's not always easy, and we can use the following three techniques to help us become more selfless:

1. Consider Others—Ask yourself these two questions: *How can I make others' lives better today? What can I contribute to life or my community today?* From this practice, we become unblocked and our actions naturally follow. Inspiration to give of ourselves and resources to other people may come instantly or as our day progresses.

2. Give Back—Try to consciously take actions that are considerate of other people, such as simply holding the door for somebody, listening to somebody without judgment, and or helping them in another way. The possibilities are endless and if you explore how to give rather than to get, your entire existence will change. This is a spiritual truth and the key to an abundant life!

3. Let Go—When selfishness arises in your thoughts, say, *I see the selfishness, I accept it, and I am letting the selfishness go*. The sooner you acknowledge the selfish thought, the easier it will be to let it go and begin focusing on how to contribute to your family, friends, society, and this world.

When we move away from thinking about ourselves by practicing thinking about and acting on how we can give, we will see our problems melt away, one by one. This is a spiritual truth. We will receive what we need when we give others what they need and we will gain our real sense of purpose without much searching on our part when we focus on contributing to this world rather than taking from it.

8: Trading Fear For Courage

Fear Is A Four-Letter Word For Delusion

When the prospect that I have nothing to distract me approaches, I immediately begin scrambling to find something to do. For example, when I have no grand plans for a nice vacation destination, hosting an evening at my place with friends, or a fine dining experience out, I tend to cycle through acting on less attractive yet mildly exciting plans. I'll start to think of going on a hike or how I should join the gym again, vowing that I'm going to stick with it, this time, I swear! Then the laziness settles in and I start thinking of household tasks to complete. I'll clean up the dishes and do some laundry so I can gain a sense of accomplishment, which settles down the fear of having nothing to do as well as settling the fear of being alone with my thoughts.

When I try to distract myself in this way, thoughts

arise of how I should be doing something more important, and how I am wasting valuable time (which I don't have to waste). Then I wonder what the point of the time I have is and what my purpose in life is. Past those thoughts is a great fear of the unknown; a feeling that loneliness will consume me and there will be no way out—that life is pointless and I am alone. The thought that everything I do is ultimately meaningless is terrifying to me. It gives me a sense of hopelessness, which can progress to a sense that a black hole of nothingness is coming, which cannot be filled—and that there is no point to try to fill it. This state is what I run from, over and over. I never allow myself to fall into that place. I'll do anything to stay out of it. It's the greatest fear I have. I keep my distance from it. It never occurs to me that if I feel such a sense of emptiness and loneliness, that I will be okay.

What if I applied the same process I use with my thoughts to that fear? What if I say in my mind, *I see the fear, I accept the fear, and I am letting the fear go*? What if I applied this to any fear? Maybe my fear is of climbing a ladder that I need to climb. Maybe the fear is speaking in front of a crowd of people. Whatever the fear is, I have found that the solution is so simple that I have a difficult time accepting it. Honesty helps with this lack of acceptance. I know the spiritual truth about fear and this brings acceptance about the solution and the fear itself.

Fear is underneath resentment, guilt, and selfishness. It's also under dishonesty. Why would I ever lie to myself or anybody else? There is only one reason: fear. Why would I resent, think selfishly, or be guilty? Again, the reason is fear! I might have a fear that I will lose something or not get something.

There is a cycle to be aware of here. When we resent somebody, it is due to fear that they may harm us further. To try and balance this, we tend to act out in anger (either silently or outwardly), which causes distance in the relationship and ill feelings in the other person. We feel guilt for causing harm and under that guilt is the fear of rejection. To try and balance this, we tend to people-please by ensuring we give the other person what they want (or what we think they want) while neglecting our own boundaries. Eventually, we become resentful again because we feel like we are being taking advantage of. Thus starts the cycle of fear all over again. Now, we can clearly see that we are creating our own fear!

The key to overcoming fear is being honest with ourselves, first. Remember, fears are just thoughts, to begin with. Then the emotions come. Then the actions follow. If we deal with the thoughts in a healthy way, the emotions and actions will follow all by themselves in a much better way.

Most of my life, I have been unaware of the fear cycle. I was consumed with fear after fear, which became immobilizing. One was the fear of rejection. This is a biggie for many of us! Another biggie is a fear of death, which I avoid thinking about, as much as possible. Then there's the fear of whether or not the world will survive, with all that's going on in it. That's a scary thought and it has many scary outcomes. Just watch the news for 10 minutes. It's the scariest horror movie I have ever watched. Then there are other thoughts/fears I have, including these questions: What if I bomb my presentation next week? What if I become sick from one of the many diseases out there? What if my kids get hurt? What if I fail? What if they hurt me? What if I never get another job? What if—(add another thousand lines here)?

To overcome any fear, I must first become aware of it. I watched my thoughts and feelings and have learned to recognize it. This took some time. I see now that it doesn't need to take much time to become aware of my fears. I can begin right now by watching for them, then I can acknowledge, accept, and let go of my fear each time I see my pattern of distraction from fear.

If we have come this far, we have already come further than the majority of the people on this planet! Let's pat ourselves on the back and rest assured that we are closer to the freedom from our self-imposed prison than we think. We have just been on the other side of something far greater and more beautiful than we could possibly comprehend. **Fear is only fear if we perceive it as fear.**

When we fear something long enough, we will end up unconsciously setting in motion the circumstances to manifest that which we fear. For example, when we fear that people will leave us if we are not perfect or good enough for them, eventually we'll unconsciously push them away from us. We'll blame that person for leaving us just like everybody else who has left us because of our unconscious actions of trying to keep them in our lives. I have proven this to myself, over and over.

The key is to not resist by avoiding fear. We can bring what we fear most to the light of awareness. Once it's brought to this light, it dissipates into nothing and loses all of its power. To find the truth behind any fear, we can write briefly what the fear is and then write why we have it. It may take a few tries, to get to the root of the fear. To help with this, we can discuss the fear with a trusted person. We need to be honest with ourselves if we are to overcome fear because it usually began with a lie we told ourselves long ago, which we have carried forward with us. Once we identify the truth about our fear, we can be free of it.

Eventually, we will see that we are creating ourselves what we fear. If I fear people rejecting me, I know that I create that situation myself 99% of the time through my actions. I push people away, when I am afraid they will leave me. Once we have a better understanding of our fear, we can do something about it. **We do this by acknowledging the true root of the fear, accepting the fear, and letting it go.** We say this in our minds and we repeat this technique each time the fear arises. We honestly don't know if it will come to be or not, so we can accept the fear as simply the mind making up stories. There is no point in fearing what could happen next week or next year, as this takes us out of the wonderful moments we can experience now. Most of the things we fear don't ever come to be. Let's be honest, they just don't!

My viewpoint on something I fear is quite limited. Whenever I need to know how limited my point of view is, I place my hands up to my eyes and make binoculars with my hands and then look around. I can only see a fraction of reality. Once I remove my hands from my eyes, I can see a much larger picture, in all directions. This exercise lets me know that I'm relying on my limited viewpoint and that there is a much bigger reality—far more intelligent than my little made-up fear. Patience and not reacting to the fear almost always gives me the room to see the fear didn't come to pass.

I know that each and every time that I sit quietly while acknowledging, accepting, then letting go of my thoughts, over and over, until my thinking becomes still, there is no fear at all. No matter if what I previously thought was scary, or even if there is a real threat of danger, there is no fear. This is a fact. This experience tells me that fear is nothing more than an illusion. The answer to dealing with fear is letting go of my thoughts about it and thinking of courage instead. I try to focus on doing the next right action while practicing faith in knowing that my fear is an illusion.

Fear is actually a four-letter word for delusion, and most of what we fear never comes to pass. The solution to overcoming fear is simple, although it is sometimes not easy to practice, and it can be done by following a three-step process, broken downs as follows:

1. Truth—Write the truth by asking yourself these questions: *What is my fear? Did any of my actions cause this fear? How does this fear dictate my actions? What trouble does this fear cause me?* Sometimes you can answer all four questions and sometimes maybe only one or two of them. The key is learning the truth about fear.

2. Face It—Once you can see the truth about any fear, the fear diminishes greatly. When you have the opportunity to be face-to-face with whatever the fear is, big or small, do not avoid it. This is easier to discuss than to practice sometimes. My experience is that it becomes easier to face fear the more we do it and the results are life-changing.

3. Let Go—Say in your mind or out loud, *I acknowledge the fear, I accept the fear, and I am letting the fear go.* Repeat this for each fear as it arises in your thinking.

You may have small fears or overwhelming fears to overcome, but you have your entire lifetime to practice this way of living. If you take it easy and practice quieting the chatter in your mind, you'll find that the fear almost takes care of itself.

9: Humility

I Don't Need Help; I've Got This

Identifying the need for change in my life was difficult on my own. I used my own limited and distorted resources to try and solve my thinking problems. The results ended up being the same each time—I never moved past my problems to a real, lasting solution. When resentment toward another person arose within me, I could only see my truth about it. My truth is only a part of the story. The same goes for guilt, selfishness, and the fear that goes along with them. Eventually, I needed to find another way to see the truth. The first realization I had was that I needed to be completely honest with myself. When I could not let a thought process go, I needed to acknowledge that I couldn't let it go on my own. There are two powers that are greater than me that can help me to let go of spiritually-draining thought processes and the actions that follow them. One power is my inner hidden resource, which is the quiet voice. The other is another human being. By utilizing these two powers in my daily life, I have accessed greater knowledge and strength to let go and do the next right action. The act of being completely honest with ourselves, followed by the action of asking for help from the two powers at our disposal cultivates humility. Humility is simply having honest views about us and our abilities while acting in harmony with these truths.

Humility gets a bad rap in today's society. The ignorant view about humility is that it means we are not strong enough to stand on our own two feet. Society says that we must be martyrs and do it all on our own! How fun is that? It's exhausting and the only reward we gain from this is the very brief moment when we say to ourselves, *look at what I did, all by myself*. The truth is that other people are spending the majority of their time trying to do the same and aren't focused on how great we are.

I remember when I bought my first brand new vehicle. I couldn't wait to drive around the city, showing it off. In my mind, everybody was thinking about my nice new vehicle. For a couple of days, I felt on top of the world. It wasn't long before reality set in. I had a standard, middle-class type of vehicle and there were a thousand others just like it in the city. No one was thinking about how great I was! When I made a big deal about it, people said what they figured was expected of them. The truth was they just didn't care. Anytime I have seen somebody's new vehicle, I say my piece and immediately try to turn the conversation back onto me and how wonderful I am. I don't give their new vehicle a second thought. A vehicle is a luxury that is nice to have for getting around—nothing more. There are very rare occasions when I see a two hundred thousand dollar sports care and actually say, "Wow, that is a nice car." Sometimes jealousy bubbles up within me and I say to myself, *They think they're so great. If people only knew what a mess their life was!* That is about as far as I take that other person's material possession in my head. Humility says, *We have a vehicle. Aren't we lucky that we can get around with ease?* Humility doesn't say, *Look at how special I am to the rest of the world*. The truth is that I am no more and no less than any other living being on this planet. I am one of the trillions of organisms on this tiny planet that is floating in a vast universe. We're not more important than the next person. Our daily agenda is no more important than the next person's daily agenda. We have just as much right to be here as anybody else. The fact that we are alive and reading this sentence right now is a miracle. Humility says, *I am one imperfect person living alongside many other imperfect people*.

Concerning our thinking, emotional, and spiritual struggles, the kind of humility we want to cultivate is one of honestly acknowledging that we need help when we need it and then seeking that help. It's not easy to approach somebody and ask for help. This means we're vulnerable. We don't want other people to know we're vulnerable. Something in us thinks that once they know we're vulnerable, they'll use it to hurt us. The truth is actually the opposite of my experience. When somebody asks me for help with their mental, emotional, or spiritual problems, I feel honored. When they speak to me with complete honesty, revealing their flaws, I gain an entirely new respect for them because they are showing courage and admitting that they don't have all the answers.

If that is the way I view other people who are honestly seeking help, then wouldn't it make sense that others view me in the same way? We can pause here for a moment and think about our own experiences to see that this is the truth. We can ask ourselves the question, *How do I respond to people who risk being vulnerable with me when honestly seeking my help?* The truth is as clear as day: we view the other person as a respectable person who is showing great strength. When it's time to seek help with a mental, emotional, or spiritual struggle you have, remember that you're actually helping the other person. When I try to help somebody by relaying my own experiences, it further solidifies the solution for me as well as the other person. I'm also not thinking about my problems during this time, which moves me toward a more selfless lifestyle. The same goes for the person we are asking for help. We're helping them just as much as they are helping us.

When major blocks develop within us that cut us off from our spirit (such as problems with resentment, selfishness, guilt, and/or fear, and we cannot resolve them), we can ask for help. Acknowledging the truth to ourselves is one thing, but honestly relaying it to another person makes it real. We're surrendering our way of handling the problem. We're showing vulnerability and honesty, which brings our ego down to its right size. The importance of this is when our loud thinking voice is quieted, our quiet intelligent voice becomes louder. That quiet voice has the solution to all of our problems. We can also ask God to help unblock us. It's amazing what can be accomplished by saying one simple word, "Help." When we ask God or our higher self for help, we're automatically admitting to and surrendering our way of solving the problem. It's in this surrender that the problem diminishes and the solution rises into our consciousness.

Regularly, throughout my day, I ask God for help. I seek help from others when required. The rule of thumb that I follow is to use the tools laid out in this book first. If acknowledging, accepting, and letting go does not remove the block, I take it a step further by asking God to remove it. If it persists, I will ask another person for help.

Let's lay out a process that will guide us as to when we need help with letting go of major blocks within us so we can cultivate humility.

1. **Acknowledge**—When you have resentment, guilt, selfishness, or fear that is recurring, acknow-

ledge it (as it was laid out in the chapters about resentment, guilt, selfishness, and fear). Also, write the truth about it, as honestly as you can.

2. Ask for Help—Ask your quiet voice to remove the block. Usually, by this point, you can move past a lot of the bigger blocks. Sometimes you need to take it a step further and take what you have written and honestly share it with a trusted friend, counselor, member of a church, or whoever you feel safe enough with. The key here is to share honestly. When you do this, you're surrendering and cultivating humility. This is sometimes an embarrassing process, depending on the issue but the feeling is temporary. Believe me, the other person views you with great respect for the courage and vulnerability you are exhibiting.

3. Give Thanks—Once you have completed asking for help, give thanks to your higher power for the courage and strength to move toward a healthier mental, emotional, and spiritual lifestyle.

You can practice this process when you cannot shake recurring blocks that are dominating your mind. When you follow through with this during those times, you will be free of your blockage and your spiritually-draining problem.

We cultivate the human need for intimacy through honest sharing. My experience has been that every single time I follow this process, I feel lighter and free. My conscience becomes cleansed. My connection to my inner hidden resource is strengthened. The way I relate to and my connection with other people is greatly improved. The missing piece of the puzzle that we have been searching for is being put into place within us. We're being filled up spiritually. This is an amazing gift.

Next, we'll discuss the pathway to gratitude.

10: Gratitude and the Joy of Living

Is Gratitude Really Attitude?

Y ou need an attitude of gratitude! I don't know how many times I have heard this watered-down saying in my lifetime. It has lost meaning. My experience is that the attitude of gratitude follows the action of gratitude naturally. Gratitude is more than a saying and more than a feeling. It's a sense that we have been blessed or been given gifts because we have contributed to life. We focus on giving of ourselves and our time and the by-product is that we can see how much we have received. Gratitude is action!

The action of practicing letting go of resentment, fear, guilt, and selfishness through the process of quieting our minds will inevitably bring a sense of gratitude. This is the way to true gratitude. Gratitude is a sense of thankfulness for the way our life is right at this moment. It is a sense of thankfulness for how others' lives are right at this moment. We have everything we need right at this moment and that is a gift. We're experiencing the joy of living.

My experience is such that gratitude needs to be cultivated. We can take additional action to help get us into the mindset of gratitude.

1. Give—Each morning, think of how you can give throughout your day by asking yourself, *How can I help to give today?* As you progress through our day, when the opportunity to help somebody or contribute in any way to the greater good arises, act upon it.

2. Gratitude List—Daily, you can write a few things you are grateful for, or a few achievements you are grateful for. Maybe you quieted your mind for a few minutes and felt peacefulness or a release from the tension. That is something to be grateful for. Maybe you went for a walk or gave back to society in a small way. Maybe you have a job; some others do not have that luxury. A gratitude list can be written or said in your mind. The point is to acknowledge what you perceive as good. If you acknowledge just a few things daily, your attitude will make a 180-degree flip, and your life will be more amazing and vibrant.

3. Let Go—By practicing quieting your mind and accessing the hidden unknown truth about yourself, you'll naturally clear room inside for gratitude to fill you up. You almost don't have to put any other effort into gratitude. You will begin to cultivate it because you'll feel spiritually fulfilled by practicing the method of acknowledging, accepting, and letting go of your thoughts.

Gratitude is not complicated. Just like most things worthwhile, we need to cultivate it through consistently practicing it. It is not complicated or difficult to practice. The benefits of having an attitude of gratitude far outweigh the effort necessary to achieve it. Give this simple process a try for a couple of weeks and watch your life change almost magically. A grateful heart is a joyous heart. The key to living joyfully is practicing gratitude.

I'm reminded of a seemingly insignificant moment in my life that I cannot help but be grateful for it, when I look back on it. I used to have a difficult time believing that there was a higher power of some kind that I could tap into, to access unlimited energy and guidance from. I couldn't understand why so many people around the world had faith in something that they could not see or touch. I was shut off from this and it seemed as if I only had myself to rely on. I read books, spoke with many people, tried prayer, attempted meditation classes, and wrote about what I believed (and what I didn't believe in), yet knowledge of this power eluded me.

Edward Scott

When my son was two years old, while we were driving, I looked back at him sitting in his car seat. He was looking out the window, distracted. I asked him if he believed in God. Immediately he turned his head and almost looked through me, into my soul. He said, "Yes, Daddy." Up to that point, I had never discussed God with my son. The way he responded with such confidence was unexpected. I asked him where God was and he simply put his hand in the middle of his chest and then looked away from me and continued looking out the window, distracted again by the passing scenery.

That moment stuck with me for a couple of minutes and then faded away from my mind. Four months later, I read somewhere about how we can access God from within us. I have since read many articles and books as well as have listened to many people describe the same thing. I commenced practicing prayer and meditation regularly. After some time, I began to sense a faint hint of energy and a sense of peace flowing from within me outwardly, during the times I was practicing. Out of nowhere, when I thought of where to establish contact with God, I envisioned the same place that my son pointed to, right where my sternum is, in the middle of my chest. That is the day when I knew I was not alone.

The significance of that day when my son was two years old, being taught nothing about God—followed by mounds of supporting documents and experiences from other people after that day—is too hard for me to argue with. I have built the foundation of my current life from that tiny moment, and I am grateful for that moment.

11: Prayer and Faith

Who Needs Them, Anyway?

What is prayer and why is it so important for us? I used to categorize prayer with superstitions and fairy tales. Prayer used to leave a bad taste in my mouth. Praying meant, to me, that I was reduced to a lowered state of being, as I was asking something I didn't even know if I believed in for guidance and care. My default nature was to try and control my life, and to run it without help from others. I tried to do it on my own. Prayer felt like I was making a last-ditch effort to save myself from the latest trouble I had gotten into. When I thought I had no other options left to try that would solve my problem, I would pray for help. It turns out that I was right about being lowered to have more honest views about my place in this world. I was wrong about not needing to pray for help as I go through my days, if I want to experience the joy of living.

Prayer is acknowledging that I am not God. Prayer helps to convince my ego that it is not the Alpha and Omega. It is also a chance for me to acknowledge my wants to myself. When my ego is left unchecked by living in denial of what it seeks, it leads me to act more and more self-centered. Sometimes, my ego just needs to be heard by me, so honestly stating to myself what my selfish wants are is often enough for my ego to begin letting them go. As we now know, a simple method to do this is to say to ourselves, *I acknowledge the want, I accept the want, and I am letting the want go*.

When I think and act as if I am the most important creature alive, my life is miserable. The pressure of living each day as if I am the one who must solve all of my problems and the problems of those around me is too heavy a weight to bear. Self-sufficiency was one of the biggest lies I have ever told myself. No matter how much I wanted to satisfy the idea that *I am good enough if I prove that I can stand on my own two feet without help from anybody*, by trying to live as though I didn't need support, I always failed. The truth is that we are worthy of love, companionship, and joy—without having to prove anything. Living in a way where we help other people and also accept their help is healthy. As we saw in Chapter 9, this helps to cultivate humility in us. We cannot do it all alone! This is a fact for all of us.

Prayer and faith that we'll be okay (and so will everybody else that we care about) helps to open our minds to the possibility of some force, intelligence, higher power, love, God, or whatever we choose to call it, to work in our lives, to provide what we need. A prayer is an act of letting go of our way of doing things and giving it over to something else. Faith is that when we let go of trying to manage things, that they will be managed for us.

For a moment, consider what your life would be like if you did not have to try and control it any longer and knew that it would turn out just fine. Wouldn't life be wonderful all of the time? We would be free to be just who we are without any fear whatsoever. That is a large leap of faith to make. Complete surrender of letting it all go for something else to look after for us, or total surrender of our way to a power much larger than us—knowing that we'll be looked after—seems like a pipe dream. However, just starting down that pathway, even if we think that we may never completely surrender, has vast benefits.

My experiences with prayer have been beneficial. When I prayed for guidance during any situation that I feared, yet is a service to others, the guidance and comfort came when it's required. When I prayed for the well-being of the person who has wronged me, the resentment I held toward them eventually evaporated. When I prayed for the ability to be truly helpful to another person, the wisdom I need to help was there. When I prayed for strength to do the next right thing, the strength to keep going arrived. When I prayed in any way that contributes to this world, my prayers were answered.

These experiences have taught me that we should pray selflessly instead of selfishly. Prayers for my own selfish wants to be met rarely worked out well. I have tried praying for my wants. The result was that I fell deeper into my self-centered world and disconnected further from people, my inner self, and this world. I have found that when my wants are not acknowledged, they grow larger and I tend to have a greater desire to get my way. There is nothing wrong with having wants. The problem arises when I try to get them without regard for how they affect other people or the world in which we live. Actively praying for my wants without consideration for anything but me feeds my selfish side and there is enough selfishness in me already, without praying for more.

How do we pray? The key to an abundant life is in giving and striving for selflessness. The first place that we give is from our thoughts and thus our actions will follow. Praying to help others or praying for help to give is a much more effective way to pray. This takes us out of our minds and helps us to develop compassion, consideration, and connection with our inner selves, other people, and the world we live in. This is where faith comes into the equation. Praying to let go of my wants and praying for others requires consistent practice, patience, and faith that my own needs will be looked after.

In the beginning, having faith may be difficult. Faith is a continuous cultivation process. It's okay if we have little faith in the beginning. It's okay that we may have lots of faith in one area of our lives and little in another. Over time, we'll see that our needs are met much more effectively than before we began praying in a selfless way. That will help us tame our selfish thought patterns, open our minds to new ideas, and develop faith that something greater than us is working in our lives. Don't take my word for it, give it a try.

Here is a five-step method for praying that will change your life from the inside out and open up doors that you may not even know exist for you:

1. Acknowledge Your Wants—When pausing your day to pray for a few minutes, your wants may creep into your mind. It's tempting to pray for a particular outcome or thing that is favorable to you. When thoughts of praying for your selfish ends arise, you can simply say to yourself, *I see my want, I accept my want, and I am letting my want go*. Your ego needs to be heard by you. Also, by practicing acknowledging your wants to yourself is a good way to become aware of your wants versus your needs.

2. Pray to Let Go—Each morning and throughout the day, when an expectation arises in your mind, you can say either out loud or in your mind, *Help me to let go of my expectation*. This is a simple prayer that I use consistently. The result is that whatever I was expecting to go my way turns out much better than I could have planned. It turns out the way it is supposed to turn out without me becoming agitated or stressed out over it.

3. Pray for Others—Each morning, throughout the day, or at the end of the day, pray for those who arise in your thoughts. They are the ones you need to pray for. For example, we can ask for *[insert a name] to be physically, mentally, and spiritually healthy*. Be creative, as long as it's along the lines of loving and for a greater good. Do this for a few people each day and watch how serenity begins to occupy your mind.

4. Pray to Help Others—Each morning, throughout the day, or at the end of the day ask yourself, *How can I be helpful to others*? The answer might not come to you right then and there, but it will come, eventually.

5. Give Thanks—Just like our gratitude list, you can give thanks to whatever you believe in for anything you want. Again, you can be creative. The point is to acknowledge that you have been given something. An example could be to say, *Thank you for a peaceful*

day or ***Thank you for a warm bed to sleep in tonight***
if you have that luxury. The more thanks given, the
merrier you will be.

Whether or not you believe in some sort of God
or not, any type of selfless prayer—whether it's
a well-known prayer or one that you make up—
will change your thought patterns to become more
selfless. Our actions naturally follow our thoughts.
Therefore, we'll change for the better automatically just by praying each day for a few minutes.

Praying only produces change if you try it. There
is no downside to praying that I have ever found.
Even if you have zero belief in God, prayer is a
method that causes your ego to let go of running
your life. Prayer helps to convince our egos that
it's okay to let go of trying to control everything
and everybody. The ego is the never-ending chatter
in the mind that tells us we need to be perfect in
everything we do and sets us up for failure because
we can never meet its expectations. This is why
we're searching for another way of life. The ego isn't
necessarily bad or good, it just is the way it is. Our
thoughts are just thoughts and they are what they
are. It's our choice whether we want to listen to
them or not.

We are no longer identified with our thoughts. We
watch our thoughts now and choose what to run
with and what to let go. We're in touch with our
true inner selves, where sanity lives.

12: Spiritually Awakened

Truth, Love, and Power Live Here, Welcome Home

Once we have begun the simple method for quieting our minds, we have also begun the process of accessing the unlimited power of this moment, where no fear nor guilt nor regret lives. Instead, sanity lives in this place. We will have freedom from the constant dialogue in our minds. This is where love is. When we operate based on love, we are operating based on sanity. We will gain our spiritual energy here. We have an unlimited supply of it with us right now. We will begin to have a spiritual awakening.

Recently, I was at the beach with my dog. She had her favorite rubber football that we play fetch with. I threw it into the ocean by mistake and we couldn't retrieve it. Right away, I followed the process of acknowledging the loss, accepting it, and letting it go. We went back to the same beach the next day. Unexpectedly, the rubber football had washed up onshore. I was delighted. A faint, intuitive sense that maybe I shouldn't throw the football for her so close to the shore arose from within me. My thinking told me that I won't throw it into the ocean this time. However, soon enough, I did, and it got lost again. I then wondered if I went back to the beach and the football is washed onshore again, if I will throw it near the water again or if I will move up into the field and play fetch with my dog there. To play so close to the water again would be insanity, as I would be repeating the same actions over and over, yet I would be expecting a different result. That faint, intuitive sense that I had was a higher source of wisdom speaking to me.

This small voice is the voice of sanity and love. When I follow this sense, I have nothing to ever fear. This is the voice of my hidden unknown truth. This is the voice of something much more intelligent and powerful than I am.

I tend to ignore that intuitive sense or small voice, daily, with many of my thoughts and actions. For example, each night when I put the garbage outside, into the garbage container, and I do not tie up the lid of the garbage can, a raccoon will get into the garbage and make a mess all over the yard. Sometimes,

I'll think something like, ***I'm sure the garbage can won't get broken into tonight***, and rationalize that even though the garbage was broken into the last two nights, tonight will be different! I don't know how many times I've done that with many situations in my life. The next day brings another mess to clean up. If I list examples of how I repeat the same behaviors over and over, we'd be here all day.

The more I practice the simple, effective process of acknowledging, accepting, and letting go, the sounder my thinking becomes. I gain a broader view about situations and my reaction to life changes for the better. I make more rational, intelligent, and loving decisions. This causes my inside world to become more prosperous and thus my outside world follows along by itself.

Another result of this practice is that I am accessing a power that flows deep from within me. This power has become the foundation of my life. I rely on it far more than my own will, to make it through each day. I have come to know this power as a part of me. Some people call this power God. Some people call it love. There are many names for this power. I know that this power is far more intelligent, wise, loving, and greater than I am. This power is truth itself. This inner power provides everything I need to live. I have not found one case when relying on this power by letting go of my way has not provided what I need. The more I focus my attention on this power, the easier it is to let go of getting my way or struggling to get by each day. The more I focus on letting this power guide me, the greater my sense of peace, direction, and joy is each day.

I was closed off to the idea of this power for many years. I had many judgments toward it. It was only when I decided to see for myself what this power was that my life took a 180-degree turn toward joyfulness. Maybe this power is my true self or maybe it is something that is outside of me, yet flows through me. It doesn't really matter what it is. What matters is how to tune into this power that is always here with us right now. There are many views about God. Choose whatever view you like. Whatever works for us is all that is required.

The way to access this power is to practice acknowledging, accepting, and letting go, using the methods discussed in this book. I place myself into the care of this power to lead me each day. I say a simple phrase each day that goes something like this: *I give myself to you today; guide me to what you would have me be*. Choose whatever phrase or prayer you like before beginning your day or your meditation, or ending your day. Use unselfish prayer often. The more, the merrier is what I have experienced. Prayer and meditation go together like peas and carrots. They just belong. Prayer is us talking to our inner power and meditation is us listening to our inner power.

It becomes easier to access the place between

thoughts or the **hidden unknown truth** of our being. This is where sanity lives. There is no room for pride, fear, anger, worry, or guilt. Peace and love begin to flow through us and out toward others.

13: Achieve True Freedom

The 4 Keys of Spiritual Living

There are four keys to life and each is mentioned in this chapter. By using these keys, we can achieve true freedom.

The first key to life is letting go of our preferences about how the events of the day should unfold. We can let go of our preferences using the same process outlined in this book. We can acknowledge how we would prefer people to act, events to pass, and what we want or don't want. Then we can say to ourselves that we accept these preferences and we are letting them go. Rather than focusing on our preferences, the key is to focus on aligning ourselves with the intelligence and power that dwells within us. Focus on your idea of what you believe your God is. That could be your higher mind, intuition, the universe, nature, or [insert the name of your ideal higher power here]. When we focus on our higher power above everything else and doing what we believe it would want us to do, we're truly on a spiritual path. We'll see that our problems will be taken care of. When I apply this to my own life, this is a fact for me.

The second key is to focus on the solution rather than the problem. When I focus on the problem, I stay stuck. I try to control the problem and solving it becomes a much greater task. This affects my serenity and joy of living. When I focus on the problem, my fear grows and it becomes a much larger problem in my mind than the actual truth of the opportunity we have to grow and create something beautiful. **Remember, we only have a problem if we think we have a problem.**

When I change my focus to the solution, my problem appears smaller and my fear diminishes. My peace of mind is re-established and I can think on a much higher level of consciousness. The more I view the problem as an opportunity to grow or create something better, the more my hidden unknown wisdom will provide the solution for me. The solution will become larger than the problem and I will find enjoyment in the opportunity. This is a truth for us.

When what looks like a problem arises, focus immediately on the opportunity. Focus on anything positive. Do not look back at the problem. Continue letting go of the thoughts about the problem. The more you let go, the more the solution will automatically come into focus. Simply acknowledge, accept, and let go of any thoughts about the problem and the solution will present itself. Finally, give thanks to your inner power for this opportunity. All of this can sometimes be difficult to do but if you persist, the solution will prevail and your mind will stay peaceful throughout the process.

When I focus on the solution rather than the problem, my problems almost seem to take care of themselves. That has been my experience. When we can place something else that is flawless, pure love, intelligence, truth, and inherently good in a higher status of importance than ourselves and strive to do what we believe it wants, we move away from our problems. We think less of our wants. We connect to the world and its people. We're no longer the center of our reality or the one who needs to solve all of our problems. We're free from the stress of carrying the weight of our lives all by ourselves.

Whether we fully believe that there is a God or not means little. What counts until we know for ourselves is that we try to believe in something, no matter how limited it is. If we believe we're the center of our reality, we'll continue shouldering all of the burdens of our lives. We'll continue to feed our self-centeredness, which perpetuates the incessant chatter of our ego. The key is trying to let go of the thoughts about our way of running our lives. We can do this by practicing what we have learned thus far.

We can acknowledge, accept, and let go of our thoughts followed by acknowledging that something greater than us is going to look after our problems for us by providing what we need when we need it, to take care of them. Adding this practice throughout our day opens us up to the gift of life. What we're doing is letting go of our expectations about how we think life should go. The truth is that if we have no expectations or judgment about anything, we'd be living like we're in the Garden of Eden. This practice will naturally begin the cultivation of a grateful heart within us. We'll flow with the current of life rather than struggle through it.

When we let go, we naturally become in conscious contact with another key to life. **The third key to is believing in a power that is much greater than us, which is looking after us and everything else.** A Higher Intelligence void of ego that we can align with. It will look after us, if we make room for it. We can only be in conscious contact with this power when we let go of our thoughts. Where this power comes from, I don't know, but I know that I can access it by quieting my mind and sense its presence between my thoughts. It's always there and I can tune into it any time I choose to.

Rather than try to get into conscious contact with

this power (call it whatever you want) to find the strength to handle life, the key is to let go of trying to handle life by letting go of your thoughts about it (the first key). When we let go of our preferences about how our lives should be, then we'll be in conscious contact with this power (the second key). It will flow through and out of us. Life will then begin to appear to look after itself. Our lives will begin to appear as an amazing gift. **The fourth key is realizing this truth.**

By using all four keys of life, we will achieve true freedom.

14: Daily Practice

The Sum Is Greater Than
Its Individual Parts

Establishing a routine for your daily spiritual practice will help you to stay on your journey. The more you practice, the more you get to experience the benefits of accessing your hidden unknown truth. Whether you know, think, or hope that practicing the techniques described in this guide work or not, you can only benefit from them if you practice them. It is okay if you don't master them all and it is okay to begin slowly. Any step you take to becoming closer to your inner source of power and wisdom is a step in the right direction toward what you have been seeking!

Let's sum up all of the techniques that have been discussed thus far and add a couple of extras into your daily spiritual journey.

Edward Scott

1. Get Comfortable—Close your eyes and sit comfortably anywhere. Sit as relaxed as you can.

2. Prayer—Begin each day with a few unselfish prayers or affirmations by asking your inner self (or God) for the willingness and power to be free of selfishness, fear, guilt, and resentment. A simple prayer that I use is: *I give myself to you today; guide me to what you would have me be*. Then pray for help to let go of your wants, for the well-being of others, and how to be helpful to others

3. Set the Stage—Keep this simple, by telling yourself, *I have absolutely nothing to do other than be here right now*. If desired, set a timer for 5 to 20 minutes to help get used to having this time for meditation.

4. Breathe—Inhale while focusing on the feeling of your breath entering your body. Feel the cool air passing by your lips or nostrils and entering your lungs. Exhale while focusing on the feeling of warmth flowing out through your lips or nostrils.

5. Let Go—When you notice yourself thinking rather than focusing on breathing, say in your mind, *I see the thought, I accept the thought, and I'm letting the thought go*. You can repeat this for each though that comes while focusing back on your breath each time. When the thoughts slow down, keep breathing until all thought is gone, except for a distant background sense that maybe you are thinking. Continue for a little longer and you'll feel the tension on your mind being released.

6. Relax—Relax into the quietness and continue to experience nothing but what is between your thoughts. Continue to experience what may feel like a release from tension in your mind, which almost feels like taking a breath of fresh air. When the urge to get up and go arises, acknowledge, accept, and let it go, then stay in this place for a few moments longer or a few minutes longer. Relax; you have nowhere to go. Enjoy this peace and comfortable place.

7. Gratitude—While in a relaxed and quiet state of mind, consciously acknowledge and give thanks to your inner self for a few positive aspects of your day or life. Ask your higher source of power, *How can I give today*?

8. Throughout Your Day—You can use this technique multiple times per day, at any moment, in any place. The more you practice this, the calmer and freer you are to live on a plane of intelligence and inspiration, which will cause you to make loving and rational decisions followed by their corresponding actions or non-action. The intelligence and inspiration that you will begin to access comes from the quiet place in between the chattering of your mind.

9. The End of Your Day—When you are closing out your day, you can, again, practice this same process for a few minutes, or for as long as you need it. I typically strive for at least 5 minutes. You can finish off your day by giving thanks to your inner self for the gifts of the day you have received. You can practice cultivating gratitude by practicing giving thanks for anything and everything that you have been given.

10. Seek Help Regularly—Apply the tools that are discussed in this book for how to overcome resentment, guilt, fear, selfishness, and how to forgive. This will help you to keep the bigger, negative, and recurring thoughts and emotions from accumulating.

This is a lot to digest if you are just beginning your journey. It's okay to test out these methods one at a time and build a routine that is simple and that works for you. No set format needs to be followed because your spiritual journey is a personal endeavor. Your connection with and knowledge of the truth is well worth any amount of effort you put into it. Take it easy and begin with what you feel comfortable with.

When I follow this simple yet sometimes challenging process (when I awake, when I am emotionally charged up, unsure of what course to take next, or before I end my day), I live on a higher level of existence.

The hidden unknown truth lies between thought. It is where true intelligence, love, compassion, joy, inspiration, creativeness, patience, honesty, courage, perseverance, and faith lives. It is available to us right here and right now! All we need to do is slow our thinking, which brings us into the present moment. The less we're identified with our thoughts, the freer we become to live the amazing journey of our lives and experience all the joy that is it. It's really that simple.

15: Continue Our Journey

Is the Journey Truly the Destination?

I'd love to end this reading with something truly inspirational but I will continue to focus on the truth. I'll share part of my own story while I practiced accessing my hidden unknown truth, so you can see the results I experienced from following the methods that have been outlined in this book.

I was practicing meditation on an ordinary day. Once my crazy thoughts began to slow down and I became relaxed, the urge to be done meditation came on strong. My thinking spiked for a brief moment, my heart rate began increasing, and I wanted to go off into my day to complete my giant list of tasks. Instead, I acknowledged the urge, reminded myself that I had nowhere to be but right there, accepted the urge to stop meditation, and let it go. What happened next was quite spectacular. I continued following the process of acknowledging, accepting, and letting go of my thoughts. I began to calm down and my thinking eventually slowed down, until it came to a complete stop. There was no hum in the background. There was nothing. I sat in this state for what felt like a few minutes. I was at complete peace. Then, the most amazing event happened. I chose to start thinking for a brief period. On a dime, I consciously stopped my thinking for another few minutes. No longer was I controlled by my mind. I cannot quite describe the peace and sense that I was in contact with something far greater than I am. I was safe and I had everything I needed. I wanted for absolutely nothing. I was in the presence of pure love. I was free. Nothing different had changed on the outside of my life; only my inner world has changed. This was proof that we can change our entire lives without changing anything in the material world.

What followed after this day was everything you have just read. My ego is not smart enough to produce such a simple yet powerful method that leads to true satisfaction, joy, purposeful living, and peace of mind. Something else is working in my life. I have since been to this peaceful place many times. It is like taking a breath of fresh air and letting go of everything that blocks the energy that flows from within and out of me.

This energy carries us through our days and it vital to our spiritual health. Naturally, we will find that our mental, emotional, and physical health will improve when we focus on our spiritual health. The pathway to this hidden unknown truth that will solve all of our problems is outlined in this book. The ideas of many people, their experiences, and a power greater than I am brought this book to life.

Practice makes better. Just try it. Practicing this way of life only requires 5 to 10 minutes a day, to begin with. Try it over and over, and watch how much you become aware of your thinking, surroundings, and the truth of what is. Watch how much your life changes. This is a simple process to follow although it's not easy to integrate into your life, in the beginning. To follow this entire process regularly requires a willingness to want to change how you have been living. It requires letting go of your wants in place of focusing on others' needs. A daily effort on your part is required. This is a simple process, but it's not easy to practice, day after day. I would be doing a disservice to state that this is an easy and quick process to perfect enlightenment. That has not been my experience nor is it the experience of many others. **Spiritual progress requires effort but the benefits of living this way of life far outweigh the effort required.**

This guide explains how to use a lot of practical

tools. It's not meant to be read like a novel. This guide can be reviewed at any time for clarification on how to follow the daily practices mentioned herein. Mark up the pages of this book with your own notes and refer to them often. Some days, you may only meditate for a minute. On other days, you may only watch your thoughts a couple of times. Sometimes, you'll make restitution for the harm you caused to another person and will do practically nothing spiritual. There will be days where you will put the entire process into action. This is all great. As long as you try to implement the tools to get into contact with your true power, you'll see revolutionary results!

I'll describe a typical day in which I apply these tools to my life. When I wake up, I acknowledge that I am not God. I am an expression of that power. I am a channel for the power of God to express itself. I, myself, have no spiritual power. Once I admit this, I acknowledge my plans for my day and ask for God to look after them. I then pray for help to give myself over to this power that will direct my life. I also pray for a few people who come to mind and for inspiration about who I may help during my day. Then I ask for the guidance about what steps to take next as well as the power to take those steps as I go through my day. This helps to satisfy my ego's wants, set my intention on selfless acts, and quiet my loud thoughts. Once I reach that point, I practice meditation for 10 to 30 minutes, depending on how spiritually connected I am on that day. I focus on my breath while acknowledging, accepting, and letting go of my thoughts. I do this until I am relaxed. Near the end of my meditation, when I am connected the closest to my higher self, I give thanks for my day, for my family, and for my higher power providing everything I need.

As I go throughout my day, I watch my thoughts and emotional responses in my body. I try to practice this often and each day. I know that when I can see my thoughts, I'm in contact with a higher power. I'm not a slave to my thinking because I'm not identified with it. Just like in my morning meditation, I practice acknowledging, accepting, and letting go of my thoughts and my emotions through my day. I pray short prayers of giving thanks, asking how I can be helpful to others, and for what I need to take care of my responsibilities through my day. This practice sets me on the path of consciously being in contact with the highest form of spiritual power and wisdom there is. Regularly, throughout my day, I give thanks for events as they unfold.

Before I finish my day, I give thanks for anything and everything beautiful, no matter how minor or grand they were for the day. I take note of any place where I could have done better during the day and ask God for help to move forward toward a solution. I end with quieting my thoughts with a short meditation. This makes sleeping a breeze. As soon as my head hits the pillow, I am clear and free to sleep well. This daily practice keeps fear low in my life and provides clarity and inspiration to me as I go through each day. It makes living enjoyable, even when undesirable events take place.

When blocking, resentment, selfish behaviors, guilt due to stepping on somebody's toes, or fear is lingering in my mind, I take out a notebook and write the truth about where I was wrong and then I disclose it to a trusted friend. If required, I make restitution to anybody I have hurt. Regularly, I search for ways to help other people and give back to my community. This is a typical routine that I follow. Sometimes, I sit for an hour and meditate. Sometimes, I write pages to completely clear my mind of the clutter that has been accumulating. Sometimes, I wake up and just go about my day. Those days are typically more stressful. The point is that I continually practice striving to implement all of the tools daily. The results are unbelievable.

This entire process is much easier to practice and stay accountable to if we have people to connect with who are on a similar path as us. It's beneficial to seek out organizations that practice these techniques of meditation, prayer, and living in the present moment. Living this amazing life is easier when we have people to share it with and the journey is quite enjoyable.

To begin—and if you're only willing to try one technique, do this one—focus on watching

your thoughts. Acknowledge, accept, and let your thoughts go. When we can see our thoughts, we're in contact with the one who watches them. We're in contact with who we really are. Practice this and you'll become conscious. The rest of the techniques will follow along, in their own time. This has been my experience. Just this one tool, if integrated into our lives, will raise our level of consciousness and set us on the spiritual path we've been looking for. To keep this as simple as possible, begin with watching your thoughts.

The quiet voice, that subtle sense we have that differentiates what is right versus what we want in any given moment, exists between our thoughts. When we listen to that voice, we've accessed a much greater source of wisdom than our limited thoughts have ever been able to formulate. From this place of quietness, the solution to all of our daily struggles can be found!

We can only experience the hidden unknown truth by applying spiritual practices to our lives. Merely contemplating how to access your inner truth will not provide the change you are looking for. You must try a new way of living to produce the desired results. There are many ways to find your own idea of God and live in communion with it. Explore! There is a wealth of resources available to you. You can seek people, books, and organizations with valuable experience and wisdom to help you on your creative journey. Simply asking whatever you believe in for guidance will help you to open up your mind and see the spiritual doors that you can choose to open.

I wonder what else quieting our minds down and accessing the hidden unknown truth will reveal as we continue on this wonderful spiritual journey!

About the Author

Edward Scott lives in New Brunswick, Canada. He is a father of one, a spiritual aspirant, an author, and a software developer. His passion is in the researching, practicing, and sharing with people how to become in conscious contact with their own truth and power that lies within.

Using extensive personal experience, Edward Scott implements Cognitive Behavioral Therapy (CBT), meditation, and intelligent prayer into his life. This experience is shared with other people to help them live healthier and fulfilling lives.

In his spare time, Edward enjoys pilot training, spending time with his son, creating new life experiences, and attending spiritual and/or meditation retreats.

This is his first book. He has plans to write more.

Made in the USA
San Bernardino, CA
04 June 2020

72709231R00064